I Can Be An
ASTRONAUT

Robin Kerrod

Artwork by

Wilfred Hardy and Ron Jobson

DERRYDALE BOOKS

New York/Avenel, New Jersey

CONTENTS

———

A SALAMANDER BOOK

First published by Salamander Books Ltd.,
129-137 York Way, London N7 9LG,
United Kingdom.

© Salamander Books Ltd., 1992

ISBN 0-517-06742-0

This 1992 edition published by Derrydale Books,
distributed by Outlet Book Company, Inc.,
40 Engelhard Avenue, Avenel, New Jersey 07001.

This book may not be sold outside the United
States of America or Canada.

Printed and bound in Belgium.

8 7 6 5 4 3 2 1

CREDITS

Artwork by: Wilfred Hardy and Ron Jobson
Written by: Robin Kerrod
Edited by: Jilly Glassborow
Typeset by: Bloomsbury Graphics, London
Color separation by: P & W Graphics,
Pte. Ltd., Singapore
Printed by: Proost International Book Production,
Turnhout, Belgium

INTRODUCTION

Being an astronaut is one of the most
exciting and most demanding jobs in the world,
and also out of this world! You brave danger from
the moment you rocket away from the launch pad to the
moment you touch down on Earth again days or maybe weeks
later. Up in the strange weightless world of space,
you carry out experiments, launch satellites and
go spacewalking. In the years to come, you might
spend months in orbit in space stations, walk
on the Moon, or even travel to Mars.

IN TRAINING

Astronauts have been flying into space since 1961. On April 12 that year, the Russian pilot Yuri Gagarin became the first man to orbit (fly around) the Earth.

The early astronauts were a select band of superfit, highly experienced test pilots. But these days you don't have to be superman or superwoman to become an astronaut. All you need is to be reasonably fit and to have the right qualifications and background, plus the right training.

Astronaut Specialists

There are two main kinds of astronauts. "Pilot" astronauts actually fly the spacecraft, whereas "mission" specialists carry out most of the other work on a space mission (flight).

If you are a pilot, you train by flying in speedy jet planes. You also "fly" in simulators – machines that look and feel like real spacecraft but stay on the ground. If you are a mission specialist, you train for the work you will carry

out in space. For example, you may practice launching satellites, carrying out experiments or preparing meals.

You also learn what to do when you go spacewalking. This is the popular name for EVA (extravehicular activity) – activity outside a spacecraft. You train for spacewalking underwater in a huge tank where you feel almost weightless, just like you do when you go into orbit.

Inside a water tank, two astronauts practice tasks they will carry out in space. Safety divers and engineers stand by ready to help.

Turning topsy-turvy, trainee astronauts enjoy a few seconds of weightlessness inside a "zero-G" (zero-gravity) aircraft, as the plane climbs steeply, then dives.

SPACEWEAR

Space is a deadly place for human beings. There is no air and, therefore, no oxygen to breathe. It is boiling hot in the sunlight, and freezing cold in the shade. Space is also full of flying specks of rock and dangerous rays.

For most of the time in orbit, you work inside your spacecraft. It is pressurized (pumped up) with air like an airliner so you can breathe normally, and the temperature is kept at a comfortable level so you can wear ordinary light clothes.

But sometimes you need to go outside your spacecraft on an EVA, or spacewalk, to carry out experiments or repairs. Then you must wear a spacesuit which gives you oxygen to breathe and protects you from the other hazards of space.

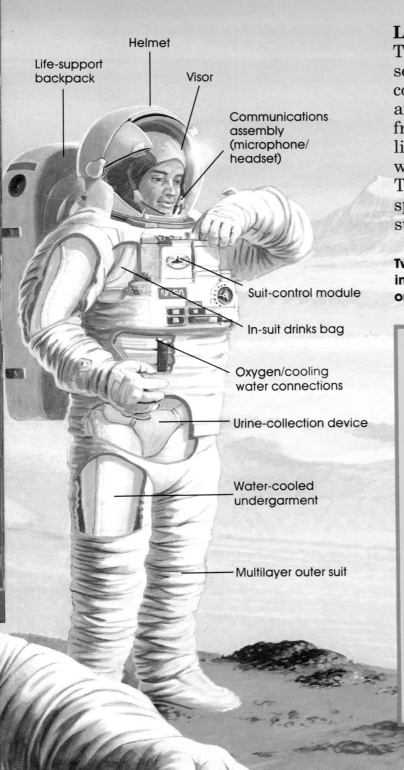

Life-support backpack

Helmet

Visor

Communications assembly (microphone/ headset)

Suit-control module

In-suit drinks bag

Oxygen/cooling water connections

Urine-collection device

Water-cooled undergarment

Multilayer outer suit

Life Support

The shuttle spacesuit is made up of several layers of fabric and plastic. It comes in two parts, an upper torso (body) and pants. The upper part has a hard frame and a built-in backpack, or portable life-support system. This supplies you with oxygen and also with cooling water. The water circulates through tubes in the special underwear you put on under the suit, and helps to keep you cool.

Two shuttle astronauts train on Earth in the spacesuits they will later put on when they go spacewalking.

Shuttle astronauts head for the launch pad, clad in their bright orange flight suits. The pressurized suits would help to protect them if an accident happened during the launch.

"WE HAVE LIFT-OFF!"

The shuttle stands on the launch pad, ready for lift-off. Inside, on the flight deck of the orbiter Atlantis, you and the other crew members are making the final preflight checks. The commander and pilot occupy the front seats; you and the other mission specialists sit behind.

The commander turns around and gives a thumbs-up sign. All is A-OK.

With just six seconds of the countdown remaining, the orbiter's three main engines ignite with a muffled roar. Atlantis begins to vibrate and rock forward slightly.

Then, as Atlantis rocks back, the twin solid rocket boosters (SRBs) light up with an ear-splitting roar. Packing the power of a fleet of jumbo jets, they punch the shuttle from the launch pad. We have lift-off!

Hurtled into Space

Inside Atlantis, you are pinned in your seat as the acceleration builds up. Faster and faster, higher and higher you go. In turn, the SRBs and the external tank fall away, leaving only Atlantis to climb into orbit.

You are now in space 150 miles above the Earth and traveling ten times faster than a rifle bullet!

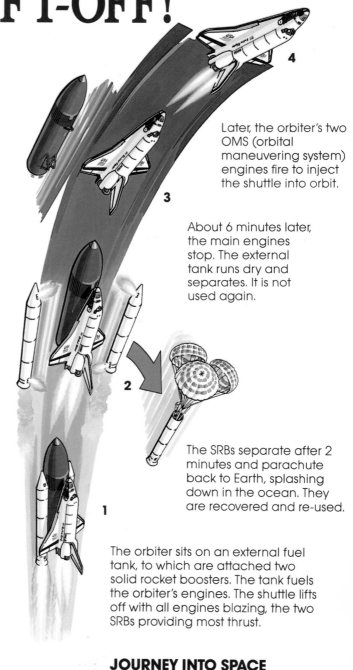

Later, the orbiter's two OMS (orbital maneuvering system) engines fire to inject the shuttle into orbit.

About 6 minutes later, the main engines stop. The external tank runs dry and separates. It is not used again.

The SRBs separate after 2 minutes and parachute back to Earth, splashing down in the ocean. They are recovered and re-used.

The orbiter sits on an external fuel tank, to which are attached two solid rocket boosters. The tank fuels the orbiter's engines. The shuttle lifts off with all engines blazing, the two SRBs providing most thrust.

JOURNEY INTO SPACE

The launch pad erupts in a billowing cloud of flame, smoke and steam as the shuttle lifts off. In no time at all, it has cleared the tower and is heading for space.

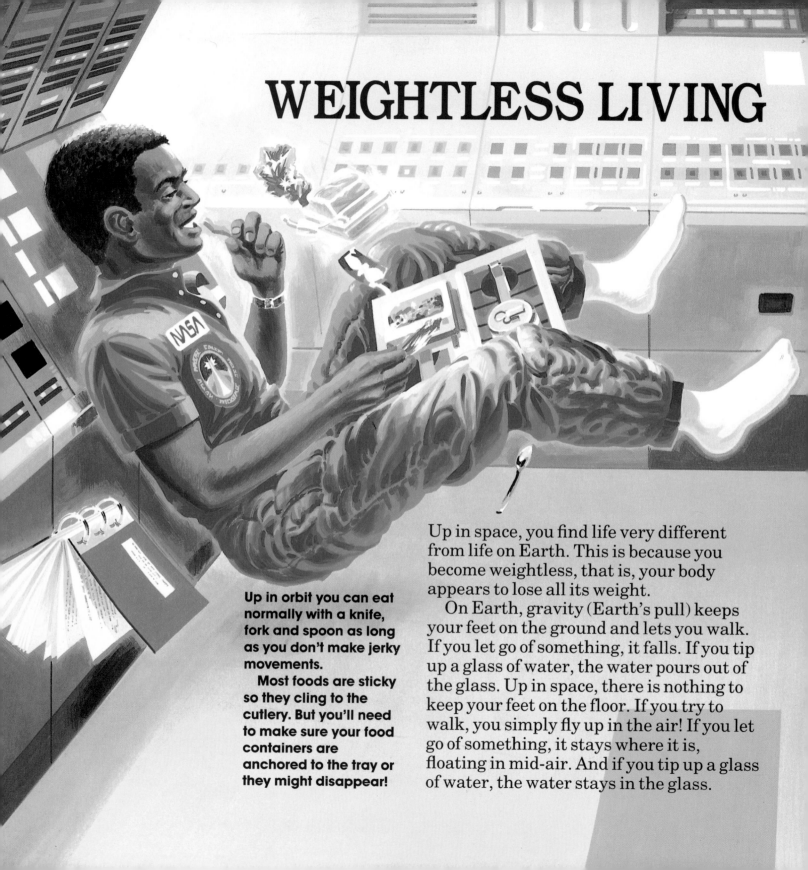

WEIGHTLESS LIVING

Up in orbit you can eat normally with a knife, fork and spoon as long as you don't make jerky movements.

Most foods are sticky so they cling to the cutlery. But you'll need to make sure your food containers are anchored to the tray or they might disappear!

Up in space, you find life very different from life on Earth. This is because you become weightless, that is, your body appears to lose all its weight.

On Earth, gravity (Earth's pull) keeps your feet on the ground and lets you walk. If you let go of something, it falls. If you tip up a glass of water, the water pours out of the glass. Up in space, there is nothing to keep your feet on the floor. If you try to walk, you simply fly up in the air! If you let go of something, it stays where it is, floating in mid-air. And if you tip up a glass of water, the water stays in the glass.

An astronaut carries out an "experiment" on the shuttle with his custard dessert. It shows how liquids form a ball shape in the strange world of weightlessness.

Weightlessness affects everything you do, from eating, drinking and sleeping, to washing and going to the lavatory.

Eating in Style
Today, space food is quite tasty. On the shuttle you find the menus really mouth-watering. You can have fruit juice, scrambled egg and chocolate for breakfast; ham, pineapple and tea for lunch; and soup, turkey, strawberries and coffee for supper. And the menu changes every day. Everyone takes a turn as "chef" to prepare meals for the rest of the crew.

Keeping Clean
You have to be careful when you wash yourself in space. If you use too much water, it breaks up into tiny droplets that scatter everywhere and give the other astronauts a wash too!

Going to the toilet in space was once a very messy business. But today's spacecraft have flushing lavatories rather like those we have on Earth. Space lavatories, however, use streams of air, not water, to flush away the body wastes. They are also fitted with seat belts and foot restraints to stop you floating away!

LAUNCHING SATELLITES

One of an astronaut's main jobs is to launch spacecraft. The shuttle carries spacecraft into orbit in its huge payload (cargo) bay. Usually, the spacecraft are satellites, designed to orbit the Earth. But sometimes they are space probes, designed to escape from Earth and journey to far-distant planets.

Some satellites are sprung into space from the payload bay like a frisbee. Others are launched with the help of the shuttle's "crane," or remote manipulator system (RMS). This is a robot arm, 50ft long, which fits inside the payload bay. Like a human arm, it has joints – a "shoulder", "elbow" and "wrist" – plus a gripping mechanism as a "hand."

Working the Robot Arm

You work the RMS with hand controllers, mounted on a console (panel) at the rear of the orbiter's flight deck. From the console you can see the arm and the satellite through windows that look into the payload bay. TV cameras mounted inside the bay and on the arm also give you views of what is happening.

During launching, you move the arm towards the satellite and grip it with the "hand." Then you gently lift the satellite out of the payload bay, place it in orbit and withdraw the arm. Finally, having checked the satellite works properly, you move the orbiter away.

LAUNCHING A TELESCOPE

When launching a satellite, the orbiter first climbs into orbit (1). The payload bay doors then open (2) and the robot arm lifts out the telescope (3). Finally, the orbiter moves away (4).

Main picture: Astronauts check out a space telescope which has just been placed in orbit by the shuttle's robot arm.

SPACEWALKING

On some missions, one of your jobs will be an EVA or spacewalk. First you suit up in the airlock. This is a chamber from which the air can be removed. It has two hatches, one connecting with the cabin, the other opening into space.

Having carried out the final checks on your spacesuit to see that oxygen, pressure, power, cooling water and radio are all OK, you can depressurize, or remove the air, from the airlock. Finally, you open the outer hatch and float out into space, taking care not to pull yourself through the hatch too hard – or you could shoot off into space like a rocket!

Tethered in Space

If you are going to work around the shuttle, the first thing you must do is attach your safety tether. You put this on to a wire running around the payload bay. If you do float away without your tether, you can't get back by yourself. The shuttle must come and get you.

Main picture: Spacewalking cosmonauts (Russian astronauts) fit extra solar panels to the Russian space station Mir.

Right: Shuttle astronaut Dale Gardner advertises two satellites for sale after successfully recovering them from orbit!

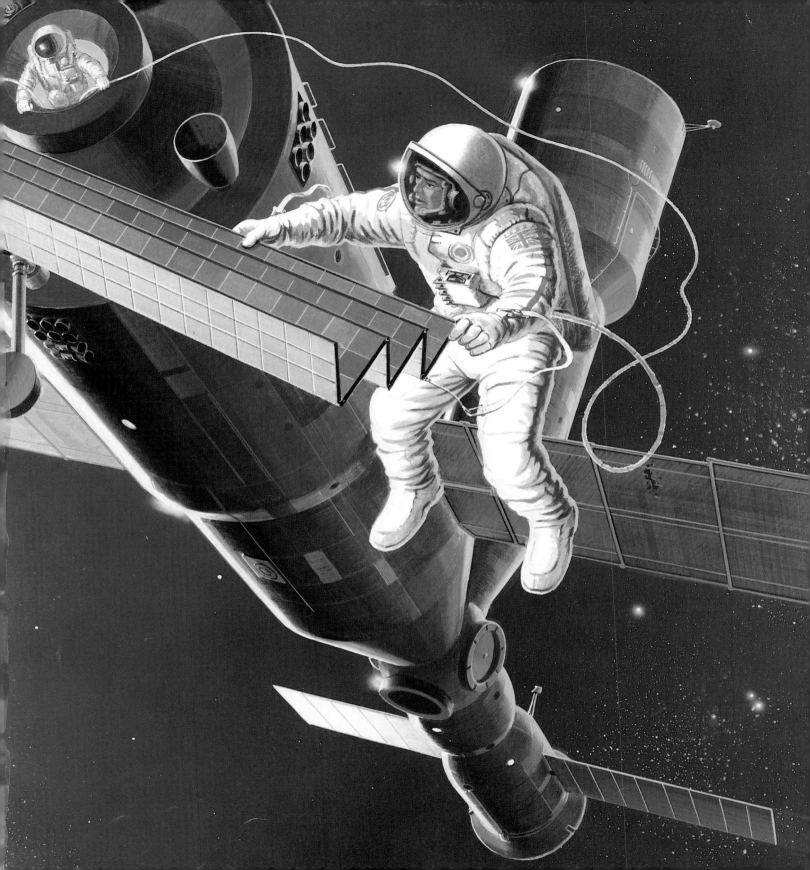

JETTING ABOUT

Usually, when you go spacewalking, you are tethered to your spacecraft for safety. But sometimes you need to travel farther afield, to examine or repair a satellite, for example. Then you strap on a special backpack and jet out into space, with no tether at all. You become a little human satellite.

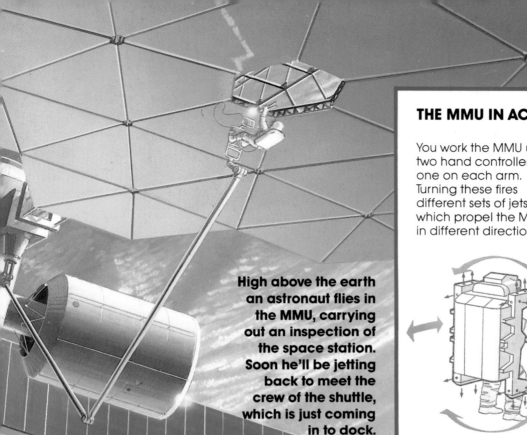

THE MMU IN ACTION

You work the MMU using two hand controllers, one on each arm. Turning these fires different sets of jets, which propel the MMU in different directions.

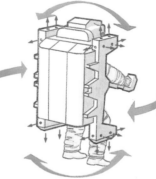

Turning the left-hand controller moves the MMU up, down or sideways (above). Turning the right-hand controller rotates the MMU in different ways (left).

High above the earth an astronaut flies in the MMU, carrying out an inspection of the space station. Soon he'll be jetting back to meet the crew of the shuttle, which is just coming in to dock.

On the shuttle the jet-propelled backpack is called an MMU, or manned maneuvering unit. The US astronaut Bruce McCandless made the first MMU flight in February 1984.

Controlling the MMU

When you work the controls of the MMU, little jets of gas squirt out from the nozzles of tiny thruster units dotted around the frame. As the gas squirts out in one direction, the MMU is propelled in the other. There are 24 thruster units in all. The gas used is nitrogen, stored under pressure in two tanks. There is enough gas to last for a flight of six hours.

In the MMU, you can jet about in any direction you want: backward and forward, up and down, and sideways. You can also spin round in any direction. If you wanted to, you could even turn somersaults!

Sometimes on your spacewalk, you fly into the Earth's shadow in space. It becomes as black as ink. So your MMU is fitted with lights so that your fellow astronauts can find you if you get lost.

With landing gear lowered, the orbiter Discovery is only seconds to touchdown. It took off like a rocket. Now it is landing like an aircraft on an ordinary runway.

DOWN TO EARTH

All too soon, your stay in space in the shuttle orbiter draws to a close. It is time for re-entry and return to Earth.

Having put away and secured any loose equipment on board, you put on your flight suit and helmet, and strap yourself into your seat. With only two hours to go before landing, you sit and follow the various stages of the landing sequence.

First, the payload-bay doors close. Then, little thruster rockets fire, turning the orbiter round until it is traveling tail-first. Next, you feel a jolt as the two OMS engines fire. This "retrobraking" slows down the orbiter, and the craft starts to fall back to Earth. The thrusters fire again to re-position the orbiter until it is once more traveling nose-first.

Re-entry

Just a half hour before landing, the orbiter re-enters the Earth's atmosphere. The air acts as a powerful brake, quickly slowing you down. Briefly, your body is pinned against the seat with powerful G-forces. Finally, the orbiter swoops down steeply toward the runway. The landing wheels descend and seconds later you touch down. Welcome home!

The tiles covering the orbiter glow red-hot as the craft slams into the Earth's upper air at over 17,000mph.

INTO ORBIT WITH HERMES

Next century you might journey into space, not in NASA's space shuttle, but in a spaceplane called Hermes.

Hermes is being built by the European Space Agency (ESA), the body that looks after all space activities in Europe. It is less than half the size of the shuttle orbiter and is designed to carry a crew of only three. Unlike the orbiter, Hermes has no main engines. Instead, it relies on a powerful rocket called Ariane 5 to lift it into space. Ariane 5 is the latest of a series of launching vehicles that have been carrying satellites into orbit since 1979.

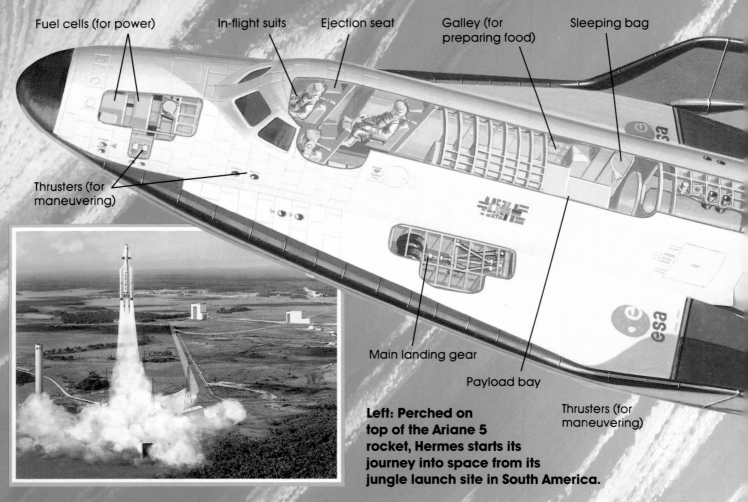

Fuel cells (for power)

In-flight suits

Ejection seat

Galley (for preparing food)

Sleeping bag

Thrusters (for maneuvering)

Main landing gear

Payload bay

Thrusters (for maneuvering)

Left: Perched on top of the Ariane 5 rocket, Hermes starts its journey into space from its jungle launch site in South America.

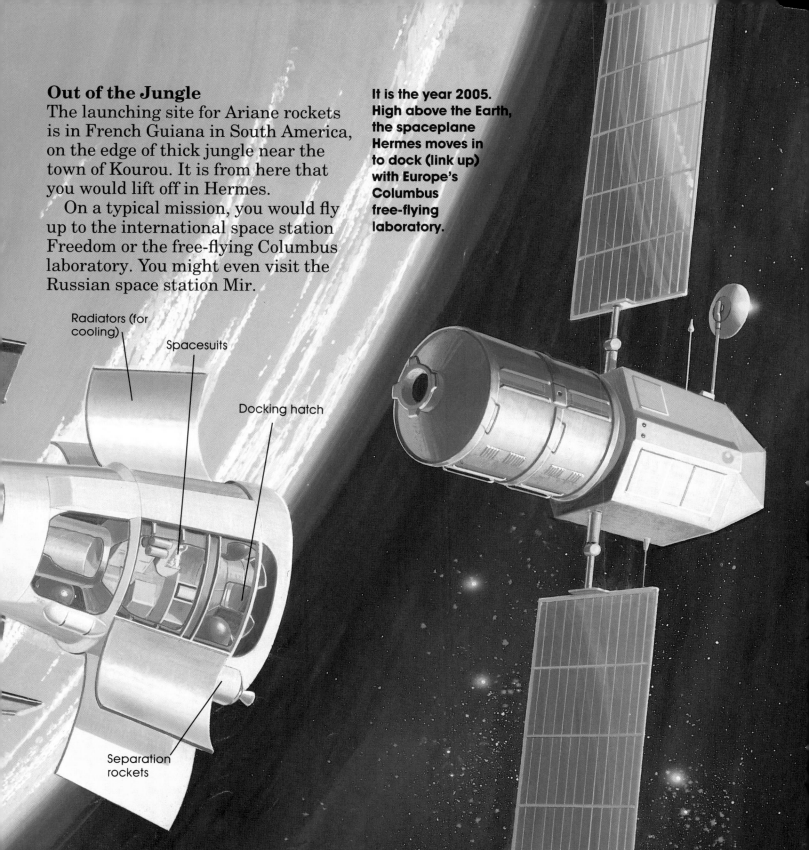

Out of the Jungle

The launching site for Ariane rockets is in French Guiana in South America, on the edge of thick jungle near the town of Kourou. It is from here that you would lift off in Hermes.

On a typical mission, you would fly up to the international space station Freedom or the free-flying Columbus laboratory. You might even visit the Russian space station Mir.

It is the year 2005. High above the Earth, the spaceplane Hermes moves in to dock (link up) with Europe's Columbus free-flying laboratory.

Radiators (for cooling)

Spacesuits

Docking hatch

Separation rockets

A busy scene at Moon base. Geologists drill into the ground to take rock samples, while miners load soil into a processing machine that extracts oxygen from it.

OFF TO THE MOON

In the next century you could find yourself tramping over the dusty surface of the Moon. You would be a lunarnaut (Moon-traveler), following in the footsteps of the Apollo lunarnauts who explored the Moon between 1969 and 1972.

In about the year 2010, you might become one of the astronaut scientists and engineers setting up camp on the Moon, preparing to build a permanent Moon base. The lunar spaceship that would ferry you to the Moon would be built in orbit around the Earth by engineers living in the space station Freedom.

At first you would live at the Moon base in converted rocket casings, covered over

with lunar soil for protection. But later you would tunnel underground and make your home there.

Doing the Kangaroo Hop

Walking on the Moon is quite different from walking on Earth. This is because the Moon's gravity, or pull, is much less than the Earth's. And when you try to walk normally on the Moon, you bounce a lot. The Apollo astronauts found that the best way of moving about was to hop like a kangaroo!

On the last Moon-landing mission, Apollo 17, lunarnaut Eugene Cernan takes the Moon buggy for a test drive.

Above: This is the view you would see through the windows of your spaceship as you came in to land on Mars. Notice the hazy atmosphere on the horizon.

MISSION TO MARS

What a busy life you would lead as an astronaut – shuttling into orbit, working on the space station, setting up base on the Moon. All that experience would get you ready for the next great space adventure, a mission to our neighbor Mars.

Mars is a rocky planet like the Earth, but it is smaller and colder and has only a very thin atmosphere. It is commonly called the Red Planet because it looks red in the sky.

Distant and Dangerous

As yet, no humans have been to Mars because it is so very far away. It never comes closer to the Earth than 35 million miles.

A new kind of spacecraft will be needed to carry astronauts to Mars and back. It would probably be nuclear powered. The trip would take two or three years, and would be very dangerous. Once you started, there would be no hope of rescue if anything went wrong. But what a thrill it would be to step down on another planet – to become a Martian!

The year is 2030. Driving a tough buggy, two scientists set out from Mars base. In the background are two supply ships, one coming in to land.

USEFUL TERMS

Note: Words printed in capital letters have separate entries.

Airlock A chamber in a spacecraft from which the air can be removed. Astronauts enter an airlock before spacewalking.

Apollo The American Moon-landing project of the 1960s and 1970s. Apollo 11 made the first landing on the Moon on July 20, 1969. Neil Armstrong was the first astronaut to set foot on its surface. "That's one small step for a man, one giant leap for mankind," he said.

Ariane The name of ESA's LAUNCH VEHICLES.

Boosters Rockets that give a LAUNCH VEHICLE extra power on lift-off.

Cosmonaut The Russian name for astronaut. Yuri Gagarin became the first cosmonaut on April 12, 1961.

Countdown The counting down of the time remaining before a LAUNCH VEHICLE is launched.

Docking The linking up of two spacecraft in orbit.

ESA The European Space Agency, the body that organizes space activities in Europe.

EVA Extravehicular activity, or activity outside a spacecraft. The popular name for it is SPACEWALKING.

Freedom The international SPACE STATION to be built by the USA, Europe, Canada and Japan.

G-forces The forces set up when a rocket lifts off and its speed builds up fast. G stands for GRAVITY.

Gravity The pull of the Earth, which makes things fall when you let them go. Other worlds have gravity too. The Moon has less pull than the Earth because it is much smaller.

Hermes The European spaceplane, which is due to fly by the end of the century. It will be carried into orbit by ARIANE.

Launch vehicle The ROCKET that launches a spacecraft. Launch vehicles are made up of several separate rockets, or stages, linked together. The lower ones fire and fall away in turn, making the top one go faster and faster until it goes into space.

Life-support system The system in a spacecraft or SPACESUIT that keeps astronauts alive in space.

Lunarnaut An astronaut who walks on the Moon.

Mir The Russian SPACE STATION, launched in 1986.

MMU The manned maneuvering unit, a jet-propelled machine astronauts "fly" to help them move about when SPACEWALKING.

NASA The National Aeronautics and Space Administration, the body that organizes space activities in the USA.

Orbit The path in which a spacecraft travels around the Earth in space. In order to reach orbit, a spacecraft must be launched from the

Earth at a speed of about 17,500mph.

Orbiter The part of the SPACE SHUTTLE that carries the crew and PAYLOAD.

Payload The cargo a spacecraft carries, usually a SATELLITE or a PROBE.

Probe A spacecraft that escapes from the Earth and travels deep into space to visit the planets and other heavenly bodies.

Re-entry The time when a space vehicle returning to Earth re-enters, or comes back into, the air. The air acts like a brake to slow down the vehicle.

Retrobraking Braking a space vehicle by means of ROCKETS. The rockets are fired forward, that is, in the direction in which the vehicle is moving. Retrobraking is carried out in orbit to slow down a vehicle so that it falls back to Earth.

Rocket An engine that is propelled by hot gases shooting out backward. As the gases shoot out backward, the engine is forced forward. Rockets are the only engines that can work in space. This is because they carry not only fuel but also the oxygen to burn the fuel.

Satellites Spacecraft that travel in ORBIT around the Earth. They should properly be called artificial satellites. "Satellite" is another name for "moon." The Russians launched the first satellite on October 4, 1957. They called it Sputnik 1. They launched Sputnik 2 a month later. It carried the first space traveler, a dog called Laika (meaning "Barker"). The USA launched its first satellite, Explorer 1, on January 31, 1958.

Simulator A machine in which astronauts train. SPACE SHUTTLE pilots, for example, train in a shuttle simulator. Inside, it looks like a real ORBITER, and its instruments and controls work properly. A screen in front shows views similar to those the pilots will see when they really fly in space.

Solar panel A panel of solar cells, which use the energy in sunlight to make electricity. Solar panels power SATELLITES and other spacecraft.

Spacelab A space laboratory built by ESA, which rides into space inside the payload bay of the shuttle ORBITER.

Space shuttle A winged spacecraft that can return to space again and again. The American shuttle craft, the ORBITER, flies into space on top of a huge fuel tank and two solid rocket BOOSTERS. The fuel tank provides fuel for the orbiter's engines. The boosters fire during lift-off and parachute back to Earth to be used again.

Space station A large manned spacecraft designed to stay in orbit and to be lived in for a long time.

Spacesuit A suit astronauts wear when they go SPACEWALKING to protect them from the hazards of space.

Spacewalking Moving about outside a spacecraft. The correct term for it is EVA. The Russian cosmonaut Alexei Leonov became the first person to go spacewalking in 1965.

Weightlessness The feeling of not having any weight. Astronauts feel weightless in space as they float around their spacecraft.

WHAT TO DO, WHERE TO GO?

This book can only begin to tell you about the interesting and exciting life astronauts lead and the fascinating work they do. You can find out a lot more about astronauts and space flight by visiting science museums that have space exhibitions. The National Air and Space Museum in Washington DC and London's Science Museum are examples.

Visiting Space Centers
In the USA many NASA establishments have visitors centers open to the public. There you gain first-hand knowledge of space activities, see astronauts at work, and maybe see a shuttle or a rocket launch.

The most popular place to visit is the Kennedy Space Center in Florida. Millions of Americans and overseas holidaymakers flock there every year. The Center is the home and launch site of the space shuttle. The first American satellite was launched from nearby Cape Canaveral in 1958.

The Johnson Space Center at Houston, Texas, is also a fascinating place to visit. It is the chief training center for American astronauts. It is also the home of Mission Control, which controls all American manned space flights as soon as they lift off. Its famous radio callsign is "Houston."

Many young people get a foretaste of being an astronaut at US Space Camp, which is held every year at the Alabama Rocket and Space Center at Huntsville in Alabama. Young people from all countries can apply to attend.

Writing for Information
You can get general information about NASA and its space centers from the Public Affairs Section at NASA Headquarters, 400 Maryland Avenue, Washington DC, USA.

Europe now plays an increasingly important role in space exploration through ESA, the European Space Agency. It has major centers at Noordwijk in the Netherlands, Darmstadt in Germany and Frascati in Italy; and ESA's launch site is at Kourou, French Guiana, in South America. But these centers are not open to the public. Information about ESA can be obtained from ESA Headquarters, Rue Mario Nikis, Paris Cedex 15, France.

Becoming an Astronaut
More and more astronauts will be needed in the years ahead as space activities continue to expand, and the international space station Freedom becomes operational. NASA and ESA have regular intakes of candidates for astronaut training.

Almost anyone who has a good education and skills in certain fields can apply to be an astronaut. So if you apply, you can expect stiff competition! It would be an advantage if you are already working on space-related projects. Another way to improve your chances would be to attend the International Space University. Set up in 1988, the university is based in Boston, Massachusetts, USA. But before you can apply, you need to have a degree and to be fluent in English and one other language.